ZIP, ZAP, ZOOM!

Story by
Ashlin Awerkamp

Pictures by
Sandra Eide

Cover design by Robin Fight
© 2022 Jenny Phillips
goodandbeautiful.com

CHALLENGE WORDS

fisherman

I am Jax.

I like to run.

I like to run fast.

I run at home.

I run in my room.

ZIP, ZAP, ZOOM!

I run past my sister.

ZIP, ZAP, ZOOM!

I run past the cat.

ZIP, ZAP, ZOOM!

I run into Mom.
ZIP, ZAP, CRASH!

Pots and pans fall down.

"Jax," says Mom, "please do not run at home."

"I am sorry. I will not run at home," I say. "May I help?"

"Thank you," Mom says.

I run to class.

I run from the car.

ZIP, ZAP, ZOOM!

I run to the door.

ZIP, ZAP, ZOOM!

I run by the bench.

ZIP, ZAP, ZOOM!

I run into my teacher.

ZIP, ZAP, CRASH!

Drums fall down.

"Jax," says my teacher,
"please do not run in class."

"I am sorry. I will not run in class," I say. "I will help."

I run at the zoo.

I run through the gate.
ZIP, ZAP, ZOOM!

I run to the birds.

ZIP, ZAP, ZOOM!

I run to the bears.

ZIP, ZAP, ZOOM!

I run into the zookeeper.

ZIP, ZAP, CRASH!

Food falls down.

"Please," says the zookeeper, "do not run at the zoo."

"I am sorry. I will not run at the zoo," I say. "May I help?"

I run in the flower shop.

I run past the plants.

ZIP, ZAP, ZOOM!

I run past the flowers.
ZIP, ZAP, ZOOM!

I run past the watering can.

ZIP, ZAP, ZOOM!

I run into the florist.

ZIP, ZAP, CRASH!

Flowers fall down.

"Please," says the florist, "do not run in the flower shop."

"I am sorry," I say. "I will not run in the flower shop. I will help."

I run at
Dad's work.

Employee of the Month

January   February   March

I run down the hall.

ZIP, ZAP, ZOOM!

I run on the tile.

ZIP, ZAP, ZOOM!

I run by Dad's desk.

ZIP, ZAP, ZOOM!

I run into Dad.

ZIP, ZAP, CRASH!

Books fall down.

"Jax," says Dad, "please do not run at work."

"I am sorry," I say. "I will not run at work. May I help?"

"Thank you, Jax," says Dad.

Dock

Town

I run at the dock.

I run on the wood.

ZIP, ZAP, ZOOM!

I run past a shark.

ZIP, ZAP, ZOOM!

I run on a ship.

ZIP, ZAP, ZOOM!

I run into a fisherman.

ZIP, ZAP, CRASH!

Fish fall down.

"Please," says the fisherman, "do not run at the dock."

"I am sorry. I will not run at the dock," I say. "I will help."

I run at the park.

I run with some dogs.

ZIP, ZAP, ZOOM!

I run by some birds.

ZIP, ZAP, ZOOM!

I run by the lake . . . oh, no!

My sister needs help!

I run to the lake.

I pick up my sister.

I run to Mom and Dad.

ZIP, ZAP, ZOOM!

Mom and Dad hug my sister.
Then they hug me.

"Jax," Mom says, "thank you for running to get your sister."

Dad nods and smiles.
I nod and smile too.

I can run at the park.
Then I *ZIP, ZAP, ZOOM* away.